GW01397890

Poison
Taming the Tongue

Dag Heward-Mills

Unless otherwise stated, all Scripture quotations are taken from the
King James Version of the Bible.

Copyright © 2008
Lux Verbi.BM (Pty) Ltd, PO Box 5, Wellington 7654, South Africa
Tel +27 21 864 8200
www.luxverbi-bm.com
Reg no 1953/000037/07
1st Printing 2008

E mail Dag Heward-Mills :
bishop@daghewardmills.org
evangelist@daghewardmills.org

Find out more about Dag Heward-Mills at:
www.daghewardmills.org
www.lighthousechapel.org
www.healingjesuscrusade.org

Write to:
Dag Heward-Mills
P.O. Box 114
Korle-Bu
Accra
Ghana

ISBN 13: 978-0-7963-0821-4

Contents

Chapter 1

Introduction

...the tongue...is an unruly evil, full of deadly poison.

James 3:8

The tongue is very vital to our lives as human beings. As a physical organ, it gives us the ability to taste and speak. In the spiritual sense, the tongue controls our destiny, regardless of our status as Christians or unbelievers.

According to Proverbs 18:21, "*Death* and *life* are in the power of the tongue..." This means that the power of cancer, leukaemia, paralysis, long life, health and wealth are all embedded in the tongue. The tongue controls death and life!

God made us in his own image. And when God was in the process of creating the earth, He spoke with his mouth. He said, **"Let there be...", and there was!**

These were creative words. They were spoken out of faith. These words created the world and brought life into being. The land and the host of animals were created. The sea, the fish, the mountains, the green grass, the waterfalls and the rivers that we see were all created by faith-filled words.

It can be argued that if human beings were made in God's image, then He has also made it possible that His image will possess this creative power. **What we should not forget is that He did not put this creative power in our feet, hands, hearts or kidneys. The creative power lies in our tongue**.

The tongue is a very powerful instrument. But unfortunately, we are often unaware of the power it possesses. It is dangerous to handle dynamite when you do not know what you are dealing with – it can kill you. Many Christians have been killed by their own tongues. We almost always take our words for granted. Many Christians pass negative comments on their own lives, without knowing the far reaching effects.

Whoever you are and whatever you do, your language must not be poisonous.

...the tongue...is an unruly evil, full of deadly poison.

James 3:8

The first thing to note about this Scripture is that it was not written to unbelievers, but to Christians. According to the Bible, no man can tame his tongue. It takes the Holy Spirit to help the believer control his tongue.

The tongue is full of poison. Poison that can kill. It is this very poison that we will be learning about in the next few pages. When a snake strikes you, it poisons your blood stream. Some types of snake poison affect the nervous system. Other types affect the cardiovascular system. When the poison hits the nervous system, many of the nerves become paralysed and you may stop breathing and die.

When the other type of poison hits the cardiovascular system, you may begin to bleed internally and externally. **Whichever type of poison it is, you better deal with it as fast as you can – or else you will be in big trouble. Poison kills!**

I remember in 1982, my class was in a laboratory at the university's zoology department for a lesson on snakes. (We had to learn about different snakes and their poisons, since we were medical students.)

A visiting lecturer brought out a huge viper from a glass container. He opened the mouth to expose the fangs of the snake. There were these two frightening and deadly fangs within the mouth.

The lecturer put his hand inside the mouth, near the fangs and squeezed some of the poison from the snake. (This is sometimes done to produce anti-snake serum to treat snakebites.)

But something went wrong during the demonstration and the viper wriggled itself loose and struck the hand of the lecturer. He had a little cut. We were so scared, because we knew this man could easily die. Luckily, he was treated and he survived. Why were we so worried? Because we knew that the poison had the power to end the man's life.

Let's say a snake poisons someone you love – for instance your father. Your father is probably the one who pays your school fees. It means that within the mouth of a poisonous snake is the ability to stop you from going to school. Within the mouth of the snake is the ability to take away the father of a child or the husband of a wife! If a poisonous snake bites a pastor, it will take away the shepherd and scatter the flock.

These are the realities of poison. **Just as we took the poison out of that snake's mouth, we can also take the poison out of your tongue. It may be difficult, but it can be done.** But the question is "How do you remove this poison?"

First of all, you have to know what this poison is and how it works. Then you can find an antidote for it. Let's now begin to examine several important types of poison that are found in the tongue. Understanding these different types will help you to know how to deal with them.

Chapter 2

Deadly Poison #1: The Poison of Lies

Lies—The Destroyer of Your Conscience

...the tongue...is an unruly evil, full of deadly poison.

James 3:8

One thing I'm sure about is that many Christians do not know the effect that lies have on their lives. This is because lying is probably the commonest sin of all. Big lies, small lies, spoken lies, unspoken lies and half-truths are all lies. I once asked a congregation, "How many of you have been involved in the sin of lying?" Almost all the people present raised their hands. People simply do not know the damaging effect of lies on their souls.

The first damaging effect of lies is that it sears your conscience. You see, your conscience is the measuring rod that keeps you in line with God.

Your conscience is the still small voice that tells you when you are wrong. When your conscience is damaged, you no longer have that correcting and refining influence to keep you on the right track.

People with seared conscience are known to have committed terrible crimes against humanity. They are callous, and no longer care whom they hurt or offend. **A Christian without a good conscience is like a nation without a police force.** That Christian will commit greater and greater sins. He will start from 'white' lies to 'small' lies and then graduate to 'bigger' lies. From there he may actually begin to indulge in criminal acts.

I once had an encounter with a classic Christian liar who had little or no conscience. Some years ago, our church, the Lighthouse Chapel International used to rent the medical school canteen in the city for church services. We needed some wooden chairs, and this gentleman was introduced to me as a good Christian carpenter who could do the job.

At the time, I was not experienced in dealing with these artisans. I trusted everybody, especially if they told me they were Christians. We paid this gentleman a large sum of money in advance.

He assured us, "I'll do a great job for you. And by the way, I even did a similar job for another church." (I found out later that this was not true.)

Some weeks later when it was time for delivery of the chairs, we went to his house to remind him.

He assured us, "Everything is on schedule and you will have your chairs in a week's time."

A week later, he appeared and said, "Listen, I'll need some extra money to complete this chair project in another week or two." Once again, this man was lying.

I said, "Alright, we'll give you the extra money you need." I didn't know that this Christian was lying again. We found out later that he had not even begun the project.

A week later, there were still no chairs. So we decided to go to the shop to see for ourselves how far he had progressed with the work. I went along with my good friend, Dr. Nosh.

I said to Dr. Nosh, "Come on, let's go and find out when we are really going to get our chairs."

When we arrived at the shop we were told the carpenter was not in. We decided to look around for ourselves. To our surprise, there was not even a single chair in the shop. We thought we were in the wrong place.

We asked again, "Is this 'Brother X's' workshop?"

"Yes it is!" they said. But there were only a few unfinished wardrobes standing around.

When we eventually saw this Christian carpenter we confronted him, "Look, where are our chairs?"

He calmly replied, "Everything is ready. You didn't see any chairs in the shop because I have taken them to a workshop near Pantang Hospital (on the outskirts of the city) to be dried." He further explained, "The wood was a bit wet, and needed to be treated and dried specially so that you would have a perfect job. You see, I only want to give you the best." He sounded so sincere, but he was lying. We didn't know then that a Christian could lie so much.

Dr. Nosh asked, "Are you sure?"

He said, "Oh, yes."

But by this time we had begun to suspect that he was lying. So Dr. Nosh decided to drive all the way outside the city to check if our chairs were really being dried.

I know this brother thought we would never find the time to verify if the chairs were there or not. Lo and behold, when my friend got there, the people had no idea what he was talking about.

"We don't even know this man you are talking about. And we have never seen any such chairs," they said.

We finally realised that we were dealing with a diabolical liar. He had been deceiving us all along, and we were not aware of it.

The church abounds with such Christian liars. Some unbelievers even have a better conscience than some Christians.

Speaking LIES in hypocrisy; HAVING THEIR conscience seared with a hot iron;

1 Timothy 4:2

Lying—That Which Hardens Your Heart

Lying is a dangerous folly, because you gradually believe your own lies. This is self-deception. This leads us to the next damaging effect of a lying tongue—a hardened heart. The Bible calls it "deceiving your own self."

...deceiving your own selves.

James 1:22

From the stage of self-deception, liars graduate into the deadly condition known as hardness of heart.

Harden not your hearts...

Hebrews 3:8

Many people are invited to church. They sit under the anointing and hear the Word of God, but do not respond or change their lives. Although some people are not born again, they convince themselves that they are Christians. Gradually, they develop the deadly condition known as "hardness of heart". This is a stage where God can no longer reach you.

God tried to reach Pharaoh. Indeed, God tried harder than he had tried with any human being I have known under the sun. He tried every method. He sent Moses, and Aaron. These were preachers, pastors, prophets and men of God. They were also miracle workers who performed miracles of healing, miracles of supernatural lice, flies and frogs. All this, just to convince one man. **God had to kill every first born Egyptian before Pharaoh would listen to reason. By the time God finished trying to convince one man, he had destroyed a whole nation.** In other words, the condition of a man's heart destroyed a whole nation. And even after God had destroyed the whole nation, Pharaoh was still not fully converted.

It is dangerous to hear the truth and lie to yourself that what you are hearing is not true. You may need some 'Pharaohic' treatment to change your mind. Haven't you heard the testimonies of so many people who got converted after all their chickens died, or after armed robbers attacked them? **When you are deceiving yourself, simple methods of communication no longer work with you.** Counselling doesn't work, preaching doesn't work, teaching doesn't work, and advice doesn't work. What may now work are the "frogs and flies" of Pharaoh.

Lies—Tools of Satan

The INSTRUMENTS also of the churl [wretch] are evil: he deviseth wicked devices to destroy the poor with LYING WORDS...

Isaiah 32:7

Lies are the instruments the devil uses to work great evil. Lies form an integral part of most wicked and bad things. There is a saying that, "All thieves are liars, all liars are thieves".

Most wicked activities cannot go on without a lie being told here or there. Dictators for example, cannot suppress entire nations without the propaganda of lies and deception, which they continually perpetrate. **Have you not noticed that wicked and undemocratic dictators do not allow a free and an independent press to operate?** They desperately need the assistance of diabolical lies to stay in power and oppress the masses.

Whenever you speak a lie, what you are actually doing is grasping one of Satan's favourite tools. You are joining hands with the devil and you are playing his game. Jesus calls him the father of liars.

...for he is a liar, and the father of it.

John 8:44

Some time ago, I experienced an attack against my church and ministry by some members in the community. We had entered into an agreement with the local government to develop a car park by the church in exchange for building a community facility. As time went on, these people who felt they had a cause to fight, attacked our property and broke into the contractor's storage shed. This led to their arrest by the police. However, whilst on bail they began a campaign of lies against me, the pastors and the church.

Although the entire project was intended to be a kind gesture to the community, it turned out to be one of the nastiest experiences for our church. As I said earlier, **evil does not work without the power of lies and deception.**

The problem with these individuals in the community escalated to the point where all sorts of high-ranking government officials got involved. These boys went 'behind our backs' and said several things to them, many of which were untrue.

As the situation got out of control, we had to go and see these government officials ourselves. I remember one office in particular, where these boys had already been with their version of the story. Their version, of course, was tainted with lies. When we arrived at the office, we asked to see the minister. We had to wait for some hours, after which we were welcomed in politely and asked to narrate our story.

One of my associates was the spokesman for that day. He gave the background to our problems with our brothers from the community. The minister listened quietly, giving an occasional nod here and there.

At the end of the narration, the minister said, "Well, I understand your problems, and I can appreciate your difficulties, but there is something I also want to point out." He continued, "I hear there is one of your pastors who claims that he does not respect me because he says I am an uneducated person who has accidentally become a minister of state."

We were dumbfounded! He was clearly referring to one of my pastors. *What on earth is this man talking about?* I thought to myself.

He went on, "I hear this pastor also said in the church, that I was seen distributing machine guns at the market to quell a recent demonstration."

By this time we were totally confused. We wondered, "What are these lies?"

I gasped, "This is not true! It is a complete lie and a fabrication." I went on, "Everyone knows that we wouldn't say anything like that!"

How can this man believe such a lie? I thought. But these liars had already influenced him.

I insisted that there was no truth in what he had been told. However, the minister went on to outline his background as a professional and spoke at length, describing some of his achievements. He also pointed out to us he had been at home during those demonstrations in question, and could not have distributed any machine guns. Unfortunately, this man had been influenced by a lie. And this lie had a damaging effect on the church's image and our integrity.

Later on, another witness disproved these lies, but much damage and hurt had already been done. We were told later by a district authority officer about the identity of the individual who had spread these lies.

The liar is reported to have said, "I was only saying this to add some spice to our story."

You see, their goal could not have been achieved without the help of lies. This is the point I am trying to make. Evil cannot succeed without the help of lies. Lies are tools in the hands of the enemy. Lies are the weapons of Satan. Do not join hands with *diabolos* – the devil.

Through experience I have come to realise that about 90 per cent or more of Christians are involved in lying. The Bible is saying that other people's lives are destroyed because of your lies. There are believers who lie as easily as they breathe.

I trust people who speak the truth. No matter what you have done, or the sin you have committed, if you tell the truth you are on your way to receiving help.

In Isaiah 1:18, God says that, "come and let us reason together, though your sins be as scarlet, they shall be white as wool. Though they may be red as crimson, they shall be white as snow". He wipes the slate clean. When you are wrong and you admit it, it changes your situation.

He that covereth his sin shall not prosper...

Proverbs 28:13

Lies—That Which Generates God's Hatred

These six things doth the LORD hate...a lying tongue...

Proverbs 6:16,17

There are six things the Lord hates, and lying is one of them. He hates lies. Be honest when you discern that you have a problem. Get help while you can. I have done it before. When I was a young Christian I went to see my leaders and pastors to help me when I had a problem.

Be honest with yourself. Correct any lies you may have told. I have had people come back to me to recant their lies. On some occasions I have had some church members tell me, "Pastor, when I came to your office for counselling, I lied to you, but now I want to tell you the truth." God will bless such people. That is the beginning of something new. By God's standards it is always better to speak the truth and face the consequences. What is it that you have to say? Say it. Be bold, and be strong. That is the beginning of your redemption and your spiritual breakthrough.

God hates liars so much that He has decided to put them all together in one place – Hell. Liars are lined up together with sorcerers, murderers, and abominable people, and sent into Hell. Most Christians will not have anything to do with sorcery and witchcraft, but I know many Christians who would very easily tell lies.

...the abominable, and murderers...and sorcerers... and All liars, shall have their part in the lake which burneth with fire and brimstone...

Revelation 21:8

Chapter 3

Deadly Poison #2: Flattery

For neither at any time used we FLATTERING words...

1 Thessalonians 2:5

T he word "to flatter" means "to *excessively* praise someone *insincerely* in order to *gain favour* for yourself." Many leaders are surrounded by people who flatter them. They speak words which are not true in order to feed their ego. They make the leader feel that he is the greatest and the best. "There is no one like you," they say.

...A FLATTERING mouth worketh ruin.

Proverbs 26:28

It is not only secular leaders who fall prey to flattering hypocrites. Christian leaders are also subject to the insincerity of such people. What then is the effect of flattery? The answer is destruction and ruin.

In Ghana, where I live there are traditional chiefs and rulers who do not wield "real" political power. During traditional gatherings such as festivals, there are official flatterers who double as linguists to hail the chiefs and say many great things about them. Some of the accolades are so fantastic that it just makes you wonder! Many of these chiefs are even made to feel like God himself.

I want to show you some of the amazing words of praise that are showered on some of these chiefs. The first one is (and I'm using the Ashanti language here):

Ɔkonini, wo na wo twere ebo ma ebo pae.

This means, **"Great warrior, you are the one who leans on a rock and make it break."** Let's ask ourselves now, who can lean on a rock and make it break?

Another flattering phrase is:

Ɔhene kese, wo na wo tia nsuo mu ma nsuo we.

This also means, **"Great king, you are the one who steps in water and make it dry up."** Let's ask ourselves again, who on earth can step in water and cause it to immediately dry up. Once again, human beings are made to feel 'super human'.

Another amazing flattery is: Wo na wode kenten kɔ nsuo trenee ano ede nsuo ba fie.

This means, **"You are the one who goes to fetch water from the river with a basket."** Imagine that! Fetching water with a basket! Who on earth can do that?

Another incredible utterance of flattery is:

Wo na wode wo nsapan ekum gyata.

This means, **"You are the one who kills the lion with your bare hands."** Think about that! Killing a lion with your bare hands! Only people like Samson could do that, and that by the anointing!

What is the effect of all this flattery? You see, flattery is one of the deadly poisons of the tongue. It makes you think that you are what you are not. **Flattery is an injection of pride. Therefore, flattery is a trap leading to a "fall".** Because "pride goeth before a fall".

It makes ordinary men think they are God. But no man is a god. All men are mortal. That is why great kings and princesses are here today and gone tomorrow. Mighty billionaires who have everything are also here today and gone tomorrow.

Your fathers, where are they?...do they live for ever?

Zechariah 1:5

Remember the story of Herod in the New Testament. He was a good speaker and a powerful orator.

And upon a set day Herod, arrayed in royal apparel, sat upon his throne, and made an oration unto them. AND THE PEOPLE GAVE A SHOUT, SAYING, IT IS THE VOICE OF A GOD, AND NOT OF A MAN. And immediately the angel of the Lord smote him, because he gave not God the glory: and he was eaten of worms...

Acts 12:21-23

This man attended a ceremony and was the main speaker. After his speech, people crowded around him and shouted his praises.

They told him, "We've never heard anyone speak the way you spoke today. It was just supernatural."

They continued, "You know, if God Himself were to have spoken, He couldn't have done any better than you did, O great Herod."

They injected pride into him. Herod believed he was becoming God. The Lord had to prove immediately that he was a mere man. He died that very day.

I remember years ago, I asked one of my fathers in the ministry, "How are you able to overcome pride, when you preach so powerfully?"

He remarked, "I've noticed that when I finish ministering there are many people who give me all sorts of praises. After analyzing it for a while I realized that pride was being served to me on a silver platter."

He continued, "Because of this, whenever I finish preaching and the Lord has moved powerfully, I quickly slip out to avoid being served with pride."

You see, this man of God had learned that flattery was a deadly poison, which would eventually kill him. Remember, pride comes before a fall. Remember also that it was flattery that led to the execution of Herod.

When I preach, I do not look out for anybody to praise me. **When I first started out preaching, I was very interested in people's comments after my sermons.** The post-preaching comments had two effects on me. Most of the time they encouraged me. I realised that after some time however, that when nobody made a comment after the service, I was discouraged. Then the Lord spoke to me, "Do not look out for what anybody has to say. Just preach what I ask you to preach, whether they like it or not. You are doing your job!"

With that attitude I was suddenly liberated, and have continued to preach successfully without looking for the praises of men. After all, people will tell you what they know you want to hear. When people notice that you love their sweet words, they increasingly shower you with half-truths and lies. The flattery has begun and the fall is imminent!

> **...with *flattering* lips and with a double heart do they speak. The Lord shall cut off all *flattering* lips...**
>
> **Psalm 12:2,3**

I know of an aspiring presidential candidate who thought he was very popular. This man had people around him who told him he was the people's choice in several sections of the nation.

They told him, "The whole of the North and the whole of the West is for you."

"Really?" He marvelled.

"Oh yes. You have no challenger in these regions," his aides replied.

Then they asked, "If only we could have some more money to go campaigning in another region, that whole area would fall to you." So he dished out some more money to these political activists until they had 'milked' him of all his money. They flattered this poor aspirant into thinking that the whole country was in support of him.

This deluded and impoverished presidential aspirant eventually received very few votes. How disillusioned and shocked he must have been! Such are the rewards of flattery. And I know it is the same story for many such politicians. They are sweet-talked into spending all of their money, and they believe the lies that are told them. Flattery is indeed one of the deadly poisons of the tongue.

You must not only bewary of being flattered. You must also take care not to become a flatterer yourself. Do not say things that you do not believe in your heart. There is a punishment reserved for flatterers. God says that he will cut off your lips.

The Lord shall cut off all *flattering* lips...

Psalm 12:3

Do you want your lips to be cut off? If not, then stop lying to your leaders, and telling them things that are not true. **Let us pray for our leaders, that they may be delivered from the host of flatterers, sycophants, liars, hypocrites and men-pleasers. These people are only seeking recognition and special favours.**

Many pastors flatter their congregations. They tell them things that are not true. That is dangerous. There are times when the pastor will have to speak some hard truths, and not pamper the congregation with soft sermons. In some cases, you may have a very dear church member living in sin, but in order not to lose him you alter and sugarcoat your messages. This is common, but very dangerous because it angers God and wears him out.

...Wherein have we wearied him? When ye say, Every one that doeth evil is good...

Malachi 2:17

Sometimes when I preach, people wonder what my political inclinations are. *Do I believe in the opposition party or do I support the ruling government?* **It would be dishonest of me to declare I am neutral. Nobody is.** I do have a stand. I believe that some political groupings may do a better – though not perfect – job than some others. (And I am entitled to my opinion under the Constitution!) However, there are many people who wonder where I really stand because of some of the things I say. You see, you cannot expect me to say your evil is good, just because I voted for you. The Bible says,

Woe unto them that call evil good, and good evil...

Isaiah 5:20

I intend to preach the truth. I intend to call black, black, and white, white. You cannot expect me to say that lawlessness and injustice are right when they are not. The Word of God says,

Woe unto them...that put bitter for sweet, and sweet for bitter!

Isaiah 5:20

He that saith unto the wicked, Thou art righteous; him shall the people curse, nations shall abhor him:

Proverbs 24:24

You see, with time people see through your hypocrisy. People secretly admire leaders who are bold and truthful. The "nation" in the above verse could also symbolize the church.

...with flattering lips and with a double heart do they speak.

Psalm 12:2

21

Chapter 4

Deadly Poison #3: Profane Language

But shun profane and vain babblings: for they will increase unto more ungodliness.

2 Timothy 2:16

Profane language is immoral, dirty, indecent, filthy, lewd, or unwholesome talk. The Bible instructs the Christian to reject profane, vain or godless chatter. As a believer, profane words must never be part of your language.

Some years ago when I was working at the hospital, there was a nurse who was loaded with profane jokes. She would speak obscenities and make lewd suggestions all day long. When we arrived on the ward, it wouldn't take her long to produce some off-colour story with sexual innuendoes.

There are many workplaces like that with indecent people who try to involve you in their godless chatter. But the Bible says that this godless chatter will only lead to more ungodliness.

Profane language defiles the person speaking, and defiles the hearers as well. The Word of God says,

> **And there shall in no wise enter into it any thing that defileth...**
>
> **Revelation 21:27**

Understand one thing: death and life are in the power of the tongue. Spirituality and carnality are therefore under the control of the tongue. **You become more carnal and godless as you allow your tongue to keep speaking indecent things.** Remember that singing is almost the same as speaking. Songs are basically words with a melody. When I was in the university, there was a hall of residence which had a profane choir. They modified holy and beautiful hymns written by great men of God, replacing the original words with detailed descriptions of the sexual organs and the sexual act.

Many Christians who lived in the hall of residence which had this profane choir, have complained in later years that they found it difficult to sing some of these songs and hymns in church. They had heard the profane version for so long that during worship times, these obscene lyrics would immediately come to mind.

These students also had their own version of our national anthem. Some of you may just laugh it off. But this is no joke – this is one of the deadly poisons of the tongue.

> **...neither shalt thou profane the name of thy God...**
>
> **Leviticus 18:21**

I know that there are some Christians who need a "spiritual" mouthwash. They are Christians all right, but their tongues need a bit of cleansing.

Chapter 5

Deadly Poison #4: Tale-Bearing

Tale-bearing is another of the deadly poisons of the tongue. The Bible teaches us that it has the ability to separate best friends. When I look back on my life I remember some wonderful friendships I enjoyed. Today, some of these close friendships no longer exist – because of tale-bearing.

Thou shalt not go up and down as a *talebearer* among thy people...

Leviticus 19:16

Tale-bearing is a principal cause of division in churches. The tale-bearer is the agent who brings about Satan's purpose for destroying God's people.

Where no wood is, there the fire goeth out: so where there is no talebearer, the strife ceaseth.

Proverbs 26:20

A tale-bearer can be likened to someone who goes from house to house to deliver his goods.

...wandering about from house to house...tattlers also and busybodies, speaking things which they ought not.

1 Timothy 5:13

The Bible makes it clear that when a tale-bearer is in your midst there is always trouble. A gossip within a group can easily destroy it, whether it has a spiritual purpose or not. Sometimes a tale-bearer will create division between two pastors in the church. He will also create division between pastors and members of the congregation. This is very common. Indeed, he can even separate husbands and wives.

...*mark* them which cause divisions and offences...and *avoid* them.

Romans 16:17

I have had very close friends who are no longer that close to me because of tale-bearing. Some newsmongers came in between us and attributed things to me that I never said. When a tale-bearer becomes close to your friend, separation will gradually set in between the two of you.

Every Christian must be wary of such people. It is also important to examine your own life so that the Holy Ghost can deal with any tendency of tale-bearing.

The Bible says in clear terms that the tale-bearer will be cut off from the inheritance of God's children.

I would describe one city in Europe, as a city of tale-bearers. I know you will be wondering which city this is, but I will leave you to guess here. Where there are many tale-bearers there is a lot of talk, gossip, hearsay, and rumour mongering. Divisions are caused in churches in this city because of the existence of tale-bearers who have nothing better to do with their time. They have one story after another, which they peddle over the phone in the evenings. No wonder the work of God is stifled in this city.

A TALEBEARER revealeth secrets...

Proverbs 11:13

The words of a TALEBEARER are as wounds, and they go down into the innermost parts of the belly.

Proverbs 18:8

Chapter 6

Deadly Poison #5: Blasphemy

"To blaspheme" is "to speak in an irreverent way about God or sacred things." It also means to show contempt or irreverence for God.

And the scribes which came down from Jerusalem said, He hath Beelzebub, and by the prince of the devils casteth he out devils.

Mark 3:22

Jesus was an anointed preacher in town. He ministered under the power and the unction of the Holy Ghost. He raised the dead, He cleansed the lepers and he cast out devils. Then a group of people accused Him of being a false prophet using the power of demons. In other words, they were saying that Jesus was an occultist, or wizard.

They claimed that Jesus was anointed of the devil to deceive people. They ascribed the power behind Jesus' powerful healing crusades to the devil, when it was really the Holy Spirit at work.

They unknowingly criticised the Holy Spirit and all that He stood for. This prompted Jesus to give a teaching on blasphemy, especially blasphemy against the Holy Spirit.

Verily, I say unto you, All sins shall be forgiven unto the sons of men, and blasphemies wherewith soever... But he that shall blaspheme against the Holy Ghost hath never forgiveness, but is in danger of eternal damnation: Because they said, He hath an unclean spirit.

Mark 3:28-30

Through experience I have found out that it is not only unbelievers who make this mistake. Born-again Christians also make the mistake of blaspheming with their tongues. Can a Christian blaspheme? Yes. Look at the definition of blasphemy again. **Blasphemy is not only speaking irreverently against God. But, blasphemy is also speaking irreverently about sacred things.**

Ministers of the gospel are in a certain sense, sacred. This is because they have been *set apart* to minister the holy things of the Lord.

It is a very common thing for Christians to speak irreverently against preachers they do not even know, when all they have just heard is a rumour or a publication filled with half-truths. **Whenever you accuse a minister or a healer of being a false prophet, deceiver, anointed of the devil, drug pusher, occultist or fornicator, you could be blaspheming.**

I have noticed some journalists and broadcasters who very confidently bunch up all men of God, and speak and write irreverently about them. If ordinary men would sue you in court for slander, do you not think that Jehovah Nissi will also take you to the High Court of the universe for defaming his church?

Every Christian must be very careful about the comments he makes about God's servants. *You* didn't appoint them, God did. You have no right to interfere with God's church. **I want to say here that some people are interfering with things that do not concern them.** I liken this interference to meddling in someone's marriage, when you have not been asked to.

When I wanted to marry, I chose a young lady from among all the others I could see. I preferred her to them, and that was my choice. Nobody has the right to discipline or correct my wife for me. If I think that there is anything wrong with her, I will deal with it myself, because *I* chose her. She is *my* responsibility, not yours. Do not interfere with things that do not concern you. If I think my wife is so bad (and she is definitely not bad) that I need to get rid of her, it is entirely up to me to take that decision and implement it. Once again I say, it is *not* your responsibility. **Do not interfere where you have no jurisdiction.**

It is the same in the ministry. God has called that man of God. If God thinks that man of God is a charlatan and a hypocrite, then God who appointed him, will in his own way dismiss him. **You cannot dismiss another man's employee.** Why should you try to dismiss and destroy God's appointed servants through publications, broadcasts and poisonous words? You are making a grievous mistake! This mistake is called blasphemy – *speaking irreverently about sacred things.*

Perhaps you might think you are just passing judgement on a man. But it may cost you your life, your business, your marriage, your future and even your children and the generations after you. Jesus said blasphemy against the Holy Spirit would not be forgiven.

...but the blasphemy against the Holy Ghost shall not be forgiven...neither in this world, neither in the world to come.

Matthew 12:31,32

This also means blaspheming against things that are being done under the inspiration of the Holy Spirit will not be forgiven. Do not be in a hurry to pass judgement on things you do not fully understand. How mistaken we are when we think we are dealing with mere men, only to find out we are actually dealing with God!

I remember some years ago, a very good friend of mine was sitting in a church service and thought I was sitting right behind him. Unfortunately, the chairs were so tightly packed that the knees of the people in the rows behind were touching those in front of them.

During the service my friend thought, "Let me poke his knee with my pen."

You see, this friend should first have checked out whether I was really sitting behind him. At the end of the service, imagine his embarrassment when he found out a complete stranger who had been receiving those 'friendly pokes'!

I must say, I had a good laugh. This is the folly of mistaken identity.

You may think that you are dealing with man, but you will find out to your surprise and embarrassment that you are

actually dealing with God. What did Paul discover when he
was struck down on the road to Damascus?

...I am Jesus whom thou persecutest...

Acts 9:5

He discovered that *it was actually the Lord he had been
persecuting all along!* **Paul was a zealous and a moral
person who thought he was fighting for a good cause.** But
when he had an accident on the way to Damascus and
developed blindness in his eyes, he began to think again.

**...it is hard for thee to kick against the pricks
[thorns].**

Acts 9:5

Some people may need some of this 'Pauline' treatment in
order to be cured of their interfering and blaspheming spirit.
I can understand how people can mistakenly treat ministers as
mere men. Apostle Peter experienced this same treatment.

Peter did some fundraising in his church, and received
pledges and money in support of the ministry. However, two
of his church members, Ananias and Sapphira came along
with a lie about the amount of money they had pledged. They
discussed it at home and fabricated a story they were going to
tell the pastor. Listen carefully to Apostle Peter's response,

**...why hath Satan filled thine heart to LIE TO THE
HOLY GHOST...**

Acts 5:3

You see, they thought they were dealing with an ordinary
human being, but they found out that in dealing with the man
of God they were actually dealing with God Himself. This

32

mistake cost them their lives. We all know Ananias and Sapphira died that same day. The cause of their death was not tuberculosis, heart failure, systemic lupus erythematosus, buruli ulcer, ventricular fibrillation or polycythaemia rubra vera. The cause of death was simply lying to a man representing the Holy Spirit.

A man of God told the story of what happened to a critic who visited his church. He said this skeptic sat in the congregation and kept thinking to himself that the preacher was a con man and a liar. Then the Lord opened his eyes, and he saw a huge and a tall angel standing behind the man of God.

Whenever the man of God walked to the side, the angel would also move in the same direction. At times as he was ministering, the angel would whisper into his ear. The preacher at those points would smile and continue ministering. (The preacher himself was unaware of the presence of the angel.) This sceptic was very surprised to discover such heavenly involvement and support for this pastor he thought was a charlatan.

This vision was an eye-opener for a potential blasphemer. Listen to me, friends. Be careful what you say about men of God. You have no idea of the spiritual approval they may have from Heaven.

Some Christians may even die before their time because of blasphemy. With their own mouths, they cut their lives short. You may think that because someone is a controversial figure he must be doing something wrong. **But I have discovered that the higher you go in ministry or public life, the more controversial you appear to outsiders.** People have all sorts of amazing impressions and ideas about public figures.

Although I have always believed in miracles and healing, there was a time I was not actively ministering to the sick. When the Holy Spirit started to work miracles and amazing healings through my ministry, I was very surprised to hear a rumour that I had been to India, to acquire some 'powers'. I laughed in amazement. I have never been to India and I am not aware of any powers that can be acquired there. The only power that I know of is the power of the Holy Ghost. But once again, I realised that each time the Holy Spirit is at work there are people who will allow themselves to be used to blaspheme.

I know many ministers who have become known as controversial figures because of the gospel. The more they did God's work, the more controversial they became.

Everywhere Paul went, he was considered a controversial person. The crowds did not like him in most of the cities he ministered. At one point, soldiers had to escort him away because the crowds were so angry with him. People were filled with so much hatred for him.

> **...they caught Paul and Silas...And brought them to the magistrates, saying, These men...exceedingly trouble our city.**
>
> **Acts 16:19, 20**

Paul, also experienced much blasphemy in his ministry.

> **And when they opposed...and BLASPHEMED, he shook his raiment, and said... Your blood be upon your own heads...**
>
> **Acts 18:6**

Perhaps, if Paul had lived in our time, he would have hit the headlines in the tabloids time and time again. Many

Christians would have said, "If you were really doing the right thing you would not have so much trouble all the time."

As a minister or Christian, do not be too concerned about having people think and speak well of you all the time. Jesus said,

Woe unto you, when all men shall speak well of you...

Luke 6:26

Jesus is our example-setter. Jesus is our Commander-in-Chief. We take instructions from him. If anyone speaks against us, he will have the Holy Spirit and Jehovah El'Shaddai to reckon with.

Chapter 7

Deadly Poison #6:
Foolish Talking

Neither filthiness, nor foolish talking…

Ephesians 5:4

F oolish talking is simply the talk of a fool. A fool says all that he is thinking, but wise people learn to say what is appropriate in every situation. Foolish speaking can cost you your life.

Remember the story of Joseph when he had a dream. He dreamt that his father and his brothers were bowing down to him. Obviously, he didn't create his own dream. It was a dream in which the Spirit of God was showing him the future.

And Joseph dreamed a dream, and he told it his brethren: and they hated him yet the more.

Genesis 37:5

Joseph made the mistake of blurting out all of the vision and plan of God at the wrong time. And more especially, to the wrong people. That was foolish talking. This foolish talk led eventually to his being kidnapped and taken hostage.

There are things God reveals that you must not tell anyone. Keep them in your heart. At the right time they will come to pass. I have many things in my heart that I have not yet spoken about – it would be too dangerous.

There are many other forms of foolish talking. One common type is the endless chitchat of some ladies. You must realise that in the multitude of chatting you are likely to say something wrong. You are likely to speak a wrong word and sin.

For in the multitude of…many words there are also divers vanities…

Ecclesiastes 5:7

The women who God commends have what we call a 'quiet spirit'.

… a meek a.ᴺd QUIET spirit…is…of GREAT PRICE.

1 Peter 3:4

I believe that much speaking, especially about godless things, drains the anointing. Jesus said,

…the words that I speak unto you, they are spirit [anointing]**, and they are life.**

John 6:63

37

What this means is that the words Jesus spoke actually contained the anointing. This also means that the more he ministered and spoke, the more the anointing was being imparted. **That is why anyone serious about ministry, will conserve the anointing instead of dissipating it through godless chatter.**

The last form of foolish speaking I want to consider is speaking without giving glory to God. We must be careful to give glory to God and acknowledge Him in all that we say.

I remember the story of a man who escaped from an earthquake in San Francisco. He was interviewed on television. The interviewer asked him how he managed to escape with his life after being buried for three days in the rubble.

This man foolishly said, "I was able to survive under the rubble of this earthquake because of my strong will power."

How foolish!

A week later, this same man who claimed he had strong will power had a heart attack and died suddenly. Tell me, where was his will power during the heart attack?

Instead of giving glory to God for saving his life, he was talking about his will power. How foolish! The Bible says,

There is no man that hath power over the spirit to retain the spirit; neither hath he power in the day of death...

Ecclesiastes 8:8

Let us be careful to give God the glory for the things He does for us. Foolish and empty talk only reveals our emptiness and ignorance.

Chapter 8

Deadly Poison #7: Expressing Doubt

The expression of doubt through our words is one of the things God hates. If you study the Bible carefully, you will find out that the Lord becomes very angry with doubting children. He wants us to trust and believe in Him. He wants us to follow Him, and know that it is well with us because He is Jehovah – the one who keeps covenants and promises.

In the book of Hebrews, there is a question:

But with whom was he grieved forty years...

Hebrews 3:17

Was it the adulterers? Was it the idolaters? Was it the thieves? No. *It was those who did not believe.*

You may be surprised, but God may be angry with you because of your lack of faith in his ability to bless you.

Remember the story of the twelve spies. Ten of them said, "We cannot do it. It is not possible!" I call them the "Cannot-Do People".

> **...the men that went up with him said, we be not able to go up against the people...And they brought up an EVIL REPORT...**
>
> **Numbers 13:31,32**

Notice here, that the words we *be not able,* are described by the Bible as *evil*. Words of doubt are one of the deadly poisons of the tongue. Observe that the ten spies poisoned the minds of multitudes of people with their "impossibility attitude". There are some people who are filled with phrases like this:

We can't make it!

It's too late!

It's not possible!

It hasn't been done before!

It will be controversial!

What will people say?

It's too expensive!

We don't have enough money!

We don't have enough time!

We have never done this before!

We don't do things like this here!

I know this thing will end in a disaster!

I'm pulling out!

I'm scared!

Let's be reasonable!

We've always done it this way!

However, there is another group of people who will say:

Go for it brother!

It's a great idea!

Nothing is impossible!

It can be done!

It's not too late!

I'll make time for it!

We can make an extra sacrifice!

We will go the extra mile!

We can work overtime!

The lack of money cannot stop us!

Let's try it anyway!

I can do all things through Christ who strengthens me!

These are the types of words that Jesus wants to hear us say. We are a "Can-Do people". We can make it. God is on *our* side!

I can do all things through Christ which strengtheneth me.

Philippians 4:13

Chapter 9

Deadly Poison #8: Slander

"To slander" is "to utter maliciously untrue statements about someone." It also means "to defame, vilify, misrepresent, and denigrate another." In other words, to slander is to lie.

O nce upon a time, there was a young lady who was in a relationship with a good friend of mine. When her relationship with my good friend was disintegrating, she came along and began to narrate a long story about how evil her fiancé was. She said incredible things about this brother, making him out to be unfaithful and treacherous. However, I knew this brother and I knew that her story was calculated to discredit him.

I remember very clearly in my office, telling this young lady, "Listen, you better forgive this brother. You are simply too bitter. Secondly, these stories you have just told me about him are very damaging."

I pleaded with her, "Please, do not repeat these stories anywhere else! You will be destroying my friend's image and credibility. Do you understand what I'm saying?"

"Yes." she nodded tearfully. "I will not repeat this anywhere."

A few days later I came across somebody who had talked to this young lady. I realised that this young lady had spread her story as far and as wide as she possibly could. She even went to the extent of going to the lecturers of this young man to tell them how my friend had mistreated her. Obviously, my friend suffered a lot from this girl's slanderous stories.

After some weeks, this lady recovered from her bitterness. She came to see me in my office and said something that I have never forgotten.

She said, "Do you remember all the things I told you about Brother X? They were not true."

I was startled, "You mean it?"

She said, "Yes. It wasn't true."

So I asked, "Did you tell anyone else?"

She admitted, "I told many people in church. But Pastor, I want you to do me a favour. Could you please announce in church that all the things I said were not true?"

She was actually asking me to announce that her slanderous stories were not true!

But it was too late. The damage had already been done. And she would have to sort that out with God.

Slander is destructive, and usually irreversible. It paints a picture that cannot be unpainted. It is difficult to erase from the minds of people the impressions and feelings that are conveyed by slanderous publications and stories.

There are many ministers who go around this life wearing the images that are created for them by the secular press. The slanderous rumours of wicked people contribute to an unfortunate image of many well-meaning pastors.

There are many people who will not go to Heaven because they can no longer receive from certain men of God. They cannot even stand the sight of some pastors because of all the negative stories and slander that is spread about God's people.

Do you remember that Peter the Apostle began his ministry with a slanderous story surrounding him? It was rumoured that he had stolen the body of Christ from the tomb, and was claiming that Jesus had actually risen from the dead.

Do you realise that this story alone could keep many people from believing in Peter's message of the risen Christ? **Do you know that in his time, many people saw Peter as a grave looter and a liar?** The Bible actually tells us that people were paid to propagate this slanderous lie. They regarded him as an unemployed fisherman and a charlatan who was capitalising on other people's insecurities and making a business out of the church. Such is the effect of slanderous poison, even today.

There are some places that I have found difficult to minister, because of the slanderous stories spread by a renegade pastor. In fact, I have discovered to my surprise that pastors are best at slandering other pastors and helping to destroy other ministers.

Don't be a destroyer. Satan is the one who comes to destroy. Lay hands on your tongue, if necessary. And make sure there is no poison in your tongue.

Chapter 10

Deadly Poison #9: Backbiting

"Backbiting" means to be "bitten in the back." That is, to slander someone in his absence.

B eing bitten in the back is different from being bitten in the front. This is because of the surprise element and the absence of protection for one's back parts. The Bible teaches us in Ephesians chapter 6 about the protective armour of God. However, you will notice that there is no armour for the back parts of the Christian. That is why backbiting is so painful.

Backbiting, one of the *poisons* of the tongue is very common in divided, strife-filled churches.

Many people cannot develop trusting relationships because they are not sure about what is said about them behind their backs.

Where there is no trust there is no relationship and no unity. I don't want to have any friends I'm not sure about. A true friend is someone who says the same positive things about you, whether you are present or absent.

Wherever there is backbiting there is no trust, and strong relationships cannot be built. Once, someone asked me why a certain group of ministers did not seem to be united. Then, I didn't really know why. But with time I came to discover it was the poison of backbiting that kept everyone apart.

I remember being at a meeting with some senior pastors. We had a cordial discussion and I thought to myself, *"We are such good friends."*

I mused, "There is such love and unity amongst this group of ministers."

A few days later, I met one of the ministers who was present at the meeting, in his home.

He said to me, "How do you find Pastor X?" (Referring to another minister who was also at the meeting.) Then he continued to say some awful things about Pastor X. Meanwhile, a few days earlier we had been happily chatting together with him.

I began to feel terrible. Initially, out of respect I didn't say anything. But as the cynical and sarcastic comments flowed from this man, I interrupted and said, "Why are you saying what you are saying? **How can you say this about Rev. X when we just had a meeting with him?"**

I went on, "With all due respect, I don't think it is right to say this about someone who thinks you are his friend."

The north wind driveth away rain: so doth an angry countenance a BACKBITING TONGUE.

Proverbs 25:23

You see, people get to know the things you have said about them with time. Because very few things are secret. In the process of time everybody loses confidence in meetings and relationships. If I have something to say I will tell you to your face.

I don't believe in pretending to be your good friend, smiling at you, then turning around in your absence to stab you in the back. That is backbiting! A painful bite in the back!!!

Pastors need the operation of the gifts of the Spirit to identify backbiters. I remember some years ago there was a young lady who would minister beautifully before I preached. I trusted her as one of my loyal and dedicated church members.

One day, as I slept, the Spirit of the Lord gave me a dream. In the dream, I was fighting with her. We were trading punches like common street fighters. Our arms were flailing in the air. Then I suddenly woke up and couldn't believe what I had just dreamt about.

The Spirit of the Lord told me, "This seemingly loyal lady whom you think is one of your trusted people is a slanderous backbiter. She joins others to speak much evil against you. But when she sees you she is full of smiles and encouraging words."

Within the next few days, what I had seen in the dream came to light. The Lord had revealed this to me to protect me from the poison of this person's tongue.

One minister friend recounted how the Lord gave him a revelation about his associate pastor.

He said to me, "My associate sounds very humble and loyal. For many years this man has been by my side, apparently supporting and helping to build. I could hardly believe that the Lord was revealing something negative about this particular pastor."

He went on, "I had a dream. In this dream somebody attacked me in my house. I rose up to defend myself. This attacker had a dagger with which he was trying to stab me. As I struggled with my assailant, I reached out to grasp a black hood he had over his face.

Up to this point I didn't know who my assailant was. Finally I was able to lift the hood. Lo and behold, it was my associate.

I shouted 'Hey! Pastor X. Is it you? Are you trying to kill me?' "

Then he woke up. From that point, further revelations came out concerning this associate. He had been secretly spreading dissension and dissatisfaction amongst the congregation and other leaders.

This was affecting church growth, he told me. And it was this discovery that led to the eventual removal of this backbiting associate. My friend's church was thus saved from decline.

You see, backbiting poisons relationships and churches with mistrust and suspicion.

...God gave them over to a reprobate mind... BACKBITERS, haters of God, despiteful...

Romans 1:28,30

Chapter 11

Deadly Poison #10: Murmuring

Do all things without murmurings and disputings:

Philippians 2:14

I believe the church is an army. We have a mission and a vision. The church is not just an institution to organize weddings and funerals for people. The church is a powerful tool in the hands of the Lord for the harvesting of souls in this lost and dying world.

And the LORD shall utter his voice before his ARMY...

Joel 2:11

How can we save the lost when we are not disciplined? How can we save the lost when we cannot take instructions without murmuring?

What sort of army goes to battle with complaining and disputing ranks? An army officer in my church told me, "There is a saying in the army, 'Obey before you complain'."

Murmuring is the undertone disagreement and protest over an issue or situation by disconted people. It is something that every Christian must avoid at all costs. Christian leaders must keep murmuring to a minimum. **Identify murmuring as one of the enemies of progress in the work of the Lord.**

Remember that the children of Israel were rapidly streaming out of Egypt and into the Promised Land. God was blessing them, and things were getting better. But when they encountered some difficulties they began to complain, and this murmuring led to the termination of their progress.

I recall being invited to minister in a large church. This church had once been a leading ministry in that city. However, at the time I spoke there, it was no longer at the forefront.

I told them, as the Spirit directed me, "It is because of your continuous murmuring that the progress of your church has halted. The Lord had great plans for you. But murmuring destroyed it all."

I continued, "It is very common to hear of leaders and members from this congregation making all sorts of unsavoury remarks about their church and senior pastor."

I revealed that it was this very well-known characteristic that was responsible for their decline. **Controversial though it may sound, I told them to leave the church if they could not remain in it without murmuring.**

From experience, I would prefer not to have any murmurers in my church, even if they are wealthy or influential. I submit that the only good murmurer is an absent murmurer!

NEITHER MURMUR YE, as some of them also murmured, and were destroyed...

1 Corinthians 10:10

The poison of murmuring destroys many a potential Christian leader.

Many years ago,I attended a meeting of a church group to which I belonged. At the close of the service the pastor decided to take a second offering. When he announced it, I immediately turned to the person sitting by me and murmured, "Why take a second offering? It's not necessary." She said nothing but gave me a look I will never forget.

Suddenly my heart smote me and I realised I had done something wrong. I felt so bad that I had complained, even though it was unknown to the pastor. After the service I went up to the pastor and said, "I have something to tell you. Can I please speak with you privately?"

He said, "Okay, what's the matter?"

Then I confessed that I had murmured against him when he had decided to take an extra offering. The pastor was very surprised, but touched.

He put his hand on my shoulder and said these words which I will never forget, "God is going to use you!"

I felt better after this and I believe that the words of this man of God were a blessing to me. They have come to pass after many years!

Chapter 12

Conclusion: Death and Life

Death and life are in the power of the tongue...

Proverbs 18:21

When we talk about death we are thinking of funerals, mortuaries, buying of coffins and death certificates. We imagine standing by graves weeping and sobbing our hearts out. But the tongue apparently controls this terrible thing called death. Can you believe that?

Well, the law of gravity works, whether you believe in it or not. Our personal beliefs do not affect these laws at all.

You can speak either "death" or "life" into your life. You can also speak death into your marriage, or speak life into it. If your marriage is dying, decide to speak life into it.

Say positive things about your husband. Think about all his good sides, and find something positive to say. You are speaking life into your marriage.

There are some pastors who speak death into their ministries and churches. They are always complaining about one thing or the other. I do not complain about the ministry. I consider it a privilege to be a minister.

A pastor's wife once said mournfully to her husband, "Now that we are in the ministry, we have no privacy. The church members think that everything comes directly from the offering. We have lost our self-respect."

But he said to her, "Do not complain about the ministry. Be glad and see the many positive aspects of it. People's lives are being changed. You are involved in the most worthwhile job of all."

He told her, "Apart from everything on this earth-when you get to Heaven you will have an extra reward."

He went on, "Say to yourself, 'I'm glad I'm in the ministry. I'm glad I have an opportunity to serve the Lord. I'm in the best job of all." Then she brightened up. You see, you can speak happiness and joy into every aspect of your life.

You may think that this is just a theory, but I tell you, these are the words of Almighty God. This is the Word of the living God.

Death and life *are* under the control of the tongue.

Let us decide not to destroy our lives with any of the "poisons" we have discussed in this book.

Let the words of my mouth...be acceptable in thy sight, O LORD...

Psalm 19:14

Life is precious. Our churches are precious. Our pastors are precious. Our husbands and wives are precious. Our nation is also precious. Let us not kill and destroy what God has given us with our tongues. May we like Isaiah say,

The Lord God hath given me the tongue of the learned, that I should know how to speak...

Isaiah 50:4

Other Best-Selling Books by Dag Heward-Mills:

*Loyalty and Disloyalty

Leaders and Loyalty

Transform Your Pastoral Ministry

The Art of Leadership

Model Marriage

Church Planting

*The Megachurch

*Lay People and the Ministry

*These titles are also available in Spanish and French. Information about other foreign translations of some of the titles above may be obtained by writing to our address.